Learning to Read, Step by Step!

Ready to Read   Preschool–Kindergarten
• big type and easy words • rhyme and rhythm • picture clues
For children who know the alphabet and are eager to
begin reading.

Reading with Help   Preschool–Grade 1
• basic vocabulary • short sentences • simple stories
For children who recognize familiar words and sound out
new words with help.

Reading on Your Own   Grades 1–3
• engaging characters • easy-to-follow plots • popular topics
For children who are ready to read on their own.

Reading Paragraphs   Grades 2–3
• challenging vocabulary • short paragraphs • exciting stories
For newly independent readers who read simple sentences
with confidence.

Ready for Chapters   Grades 2–4
• chapters • longer paragraphs • full-color art
For children who want to take the plunge into chapter books
but still like colorful pictures.

STEP INTO READING® is designed to give every child a successful
reading experience. The grade levels are only guides; children will progress
through the steps at their own speed, developing confidence in their reading.

Remember, a lifetime love of reading starts with a single step!

The authors would like to thank Kaitlin Dupuis and Deanna Ellis for their help in creating this book.

Text copyright © 2019 by Kratt Brothers Company Ltd.

All rights reserved. Published in the United States by Random House Children's Books, a division of Penguin Random House LLC, 1745 Broadway, New York, NY 10019, and in Canada by Penguin Random House Canada Limited, Toronto.

Wild Kratts® © 2019 Kratt Brothers Company Ltd. / 9 Story Media Group Inc. Wild Kratts®, Creature Power® and associated characters, trademarks, and design elements are owned by Kratt Brothers Company Ltd. Licensed by Kratt Brothers Company Ltd.

Step into Reading, Random House, and the Random House colophon are registered trademarks of Penguin Random House LLC.

Visit us on the Web!
StepIntoReading.com
rhcbooks.com

Educators and librarians, for a variety of teaching tools, visit us at RHTeachersLibrarians.com

ISBN 978-1-9848-4790-4 (trade) — ISBN 978-1-9848-4791-1 (lib. bdg.) — ISBN 978-1-9848-4792-8 (ebook)

Printed in the United States of America
10 9 8 7 6 5 4 3 2 1

WITHDRAWN

Lion Pride!

by Martin Kratt and Chris Kratt

Random House 🏠 New York

When the Kratt Brothers
go to Africa,
both Martin and Chris
love to prowl with lions.

A family of lions is called a pride. This pride has two adult males, six lionesses, and lots of cubs!

"Hey, Chris, are you thinking what I'm thinking?"

"Yeah, Martin, I think so.

Let's activate Lion Powers!"

"My Lion Power Disc is in my Creature Power Disc holder," says Chris.

"Mine is in my backpack,"
says Martin. "I think."

By the time the brothers
find their Lion Power Discs,
all the lions have disappeared!

"Where did everybody go?"
Martin wonders aloud.

Chris spots the lion cubs
gathered in the grass.

"Of course," he realizes.
"Lion cubs hide while
the adults go hunting."

Martin and Chris
quickly activate
their Lion Powers!

Insert Lion Power Discs!

Touch lions!

Activate Lion Powers!

Now that the Wild Kratts
have their Creature Powers,
Chris lets out
a roar!

The lion cubs pounce
on the Wild Kratts!
They want to play.

The brothers do not realize
that playful lion cubs
can get into a lot of trouble.

Cubs use play to practice
the skills they need
to survive in the wild.

One lion cub finds
a honey badger.
The cub gets close.

Lesson one of the savanna:

Never play with a honey badger.

Ouch!

Lesson two: Never run
under a giraffe.

24

You might get kicked!

Lesson three: Never play
with an elephant's trunk.
"Watch out," says Martin.

"You might get swatted,"
Chris tells the cub.

Lesson four: Be careful on the riverbank. Hungry crocodiles might be waiting.

"Run back to the pride!"

Chris shouts.

Even with Creature Powers,
the Wild Kratts learn
that taking care of lion cubs
is hard work!

Finally, the adult lions
return home.
The cubs are happy
to see them.

Chris and Martin are rescued

from the playful cubs.

"Phew!" say the tired

Wild Kratts.